Cesar Chavez

Cathryn Abbott

Cesar Chavez

Labor Leader

Cathryn Abbott

VANTAGE PRESS
New York

Illustrated by Wally Littman

FIRST EDITION

All rights reserved, including the right of
reproduction in whole or in part in any form.

Copyright © 1997 by Cathryn Abbott

Published by Vantage Press, Inc.
516 West 34th Street, New York, New York 10001

Manufactured in the United States of America
ISBN: 0-533-11581-7

0 9 8 7 6 5 4 3 2 1

To the memory of my father,
William Casper Ott,
union ironworker

Cesar Chavez

Cesar Chavez was born in Yuma, Arizona, on March 31, 1927. He was raised on migratory farms and attended school in many different areas.

After two years in the U.S. Navy during World War II, he returned to migrant farm work in Arizona and California.

In 1962, while farm laboring himself, he began organizing farm workers when he created the National Farm Workers Association. Farm workers were often exploited and paid low wages and lived in poor conditions in labor camps.

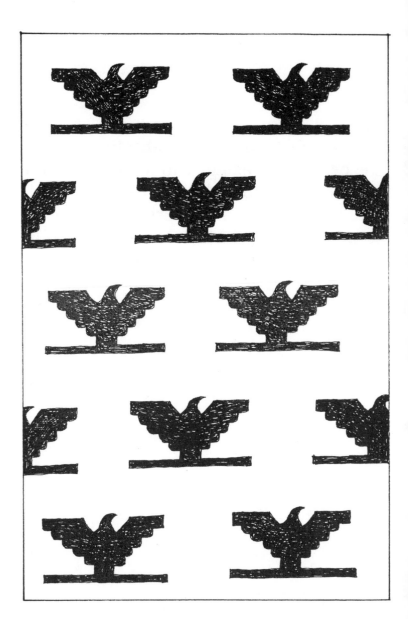

In September 1965, Chavez led California grape pickers out on a five-year-long strike and nationwide boycott of California grapes. He also did the same for lettuce and melon workers.

The black eagle is a symbol of the Mexican people, handed down to them by their Aztec forebears. Cesar's brother,

Manuel, squared off the edges of the eagle's wings. It became the flag and pin of the strikers.

In the spring of 1968, he fasted for twenty-five days in order to build a nonviolent base for his union. Cesar Chavez was a vegetarian.

Cesar Chavez was inspired in his work by John and Robert Kennedy, Martin Luther King Jr., Mahatma Gandhi, Dorothy Day, and the Berrigan brothers.

Cesar Chavez said that "the truest act of courage, the strongest act of manliness is to sacrifice ourselves for others in a totally nonviolent struggle for justice."

In a statement released by Cesar Chavez from the Monterey County jail, December 5, 1970, he said,

"I'm in good spirits, and they're very kind to me. I was spiritually prepared for this confinement; I don't think the judge was unfair. I am prepared to pay the price for civil disobedience. I am still very committed, and I'm not bitter at all.

"At this point in our struggle there is more need than ever to demonstrate our love for those who oppose us. Farm workers are wounded every day by being denied representation of the union of their choice. Jail is a small price to pay to help right that injustice."

Cesar Chavez died on April 23, 1993, in San Luis, Arizona. His wife, Helen Favila Chavez, is the daughter of a hero of the Mexican revolution. His eight children and twenty-seven grandchildren also survive him.

Farm workers still face the odds of bad weather and poor crops. But because of Cesar Chavez and his supporters, their labor is valued and recognized.